The Girls
in Bright Dresses
Dancing

poems by
Gerry Grubbs

2010

DOS MADRES

DOS MADRES PRESS INC.

P.O. Box 294, Loveland, Ohio 45140
http://www.dosmadres.com
editor@dosmadres.com

Dos Madres is dedicated to the belief that the small press is essential to the vitality of contemporary literature as a carrier of the new voice, as well as the older, sometimes forgotten voices of the past. And in an ever more virtual world, to the creation of fine books pleasing to the eye and hand.

Dos Madres is named in honor of Vera Murphy and Libbie Hughes, the "Dos Madres" whose contributions have made this press possible.

Executive Editor: Robert J. Murphy
Book design & Illustration by Elizabeth Murphy
(www.IllusionStudios.net)

Typeset in Adobe Garamond Pro & Kiligraphy

ACKNOWLEDGEMENTS

Some of these poems previously appeared in the following, whose editors I hereby thank: *Blind Mans Rainbow, Laughing Dog, Mudfish, Windless Orchard, Sulfur River Review, Hidden Oak, Red Owl, Veil, Edgz, California Quarterly, Timber Creek Review,* and *Poet Lore.* A number of the poems also appeared in a chapbook, *Still Life* (Dos Madres Press, 2005)

Author photo is by Brian Heller

The cover illustration is a digital collage by Elizabeth Murphy using as image sources: an archival photograph of women folk dancing at Grailville in the 1940s (www.grailville.org) Grailville is a center of The Grail, (www.grail-us.org) an international movement of women committed to spiritual search, social actions, ecological sustainability and the release of women's creative energy throughout the world; and Van Gogh's painting "Wheat Field".

Library of Congress Control Number: 2010930158

ISBN 978-1-933675-51-0

This book is for Mary

I would also like to thank the Great Lakes listeners who have heard many of these poems in their early stages, those listeners include K'anna, Annie, Julia, Martha, Gretchen, Peggy, Kathy, Bob E., Bob D., my good friend Bob W. and Mary, Jim and Terry, David and Gretchen, Carol, Elaine, Sam, Nannie, Ned, Amy, Barb, Kathy, Ellen, Brian and Rita, and all the others who have stopped by to listen.

Thanks also to my Xavier friends Ernie, Norman and Ty.

TABLE OF CONTENTS

What Follows

As the careful hunter can tell
From the broken blades of grass
Which way the thing
That he follows has gone
So too we can tell
From careful looking
How the thing approached
Our lives and where
It stood still
And the direction it took
As it picked itself up
And walked on
Leaving us wondering
What has been lost
And how its absence
Effects everything that follows

Lost

It is not always possible
To tell who is standing
In the next room
Nor to hear what is being said
But if the voice
Is familiar you can tell
By its tone how worried
Your mother must be
How worried you would be
If both your children
Were lost in the middle
Of a warm May afternoon

You can count the seconds
Until your father arrives
Full of anger and fear
Not knowing what to do
Knowing how precise his geometry
Must be as he measures
The distance those short legs
Could travel from the given
Hour they were last seen

How he drives through
The streets allowing
The perimeter to expand
As the minutes slip away

Disappearing like the kids
Who will have found
Their way back by the time
He returns

This is a story that occurred
Before time changed

The hours were
What they are
The minutes
Still whittled
Their wooden sticks
The shadows of everything
Fell with precision
And the word for lost
Was just being gathered
One letter at a time
From the vast field

Return

I was thinking hard
About it you know
How you turn
Down one hallway
Then another
With no mind
As to which door
Leads where
Or the different
Colors of the carpet
With no windows
To the outside world
And no string
To follow and
Not even caring
If I get back

Things I Think About

We were all gathered in the basement
Which seemed like a good idea at first

Like a man who believes
You can never have too many spoons

Or waiting for a train in Belgrade
And everything that comes with it

What comes comes
No matter where you are

Despair stands in the corner
Thinking about the next cigarette

How many times has the night come
Carrying with it the scent of the past

Each star a startling reminder
Of someone else's sudden discovery

It Comes

It comes because it is a function of words
The way purchase is a function of money
We put our words on the counter
Like a few worn coins and the clerk
Hands us what we take back to our rooms
To unwrap

The Shadow World

It was not the bird
But the shadow
Of the bird
And it was not the tree
From which it sang
Its shadow song
But the shadow of the tree
It was not the earth
That the tree clung to
But the shadow of an earth
And it was not
The molten center
But the shadow of a center
And so on
Until the whole world
Was just a shadow
Of the shining world

The Falling World

It is not as hard as you think
The water not as cold
Not as deep and fast
At least at first
When you put your feet in
Wading down until it is up
To your knees
Walking toward where the waves
Who have built their houses on sand
Come falling toward you
And you wanting now
More than anything
To save the beauty of it
Open your arms trying to hold
This falling world up

The Top of the World

If there is a roof
On this world
We can understand
The closed circuitry of birds
And how they only
Know two seasons
And why Van Gogh
Wanted all that purple
In one painting
And why I love
The smooth round
Forehead of the moon

As For The Birds

Now as for the birds
The little ones that rise when told
The ones who never complain
About the cold or the lack
The ones who have been returning each year
Who each year also leave
Whose history is written in the trees
Whose feathers have been found
Pressed into the rocks like flowers pressed
Between the pages of a familiar book
Whose voices must have been
The first musical instruments
Who have been known to darken
The afternoon and to dance together
Like a single piece of fabric
Who are too numerous to count
Who stir you to seek after the rare species
Deep in the woods as for the birds
Who can be identified at a distance
By the shape and movement of their wings
Whose colors are as varied
As the ties of a prominent physician
Who build their nests in every place
In caves and cliffs and even in the earth
As for the birds who are fed by the earths
Abundance and by the seas
As for the birds they are provided for

Standing Alone

Have you been out
On a moonlit night
Before the fields
Have grown into themselves
When they are still
Vast acres of possibility
And you can see yourself standing
Beneath the gray blue moon
In the middle of those possibilities
Not the self that is
But that other grayer self
Standing alone in the fields

Seasonal

All this time it has been happening
The stars have come out
With their elaborate proposals
The small fires have been built
On the surrounding hillsides
And the trees in their seasonal
State of dress or undress
Stand unwavering
In the thick night air

About Loss

When I get to the garden
I see the white statues
Their white hands missing

It is as if they had
Grabbed onto something
And when it started to move
They could not let go

September

Snakes start back up the hill
Even the leaves who have given all their green to the tree
Put off leaving for only a while longer
They all have someplace else to be
Everyone feels it sees it in the clouds that rush past
Moving on even now never content to be held back
Better to err in seeking too much
Even if you arrive before the others
Remembering something that makes you anxious to go

Like Water

The soul is wet
And needs to move
Over the smooth stones
To keep itself pure

Not the way we move
Over the past
Trying to remember
In a way which confirms
What we have become

Water only moves forward
Remembers only
The great sea
The clapping of the waves
As it returns

Transformation

All things point in that direction
Even the cook in her kitchen
Calming the carrots she is about to shred
Fair haired angels ready to sing for us
The transformation from one body to another

Something Green

No one has to teach the rain
How to give it doesn't hold back
Even a small share for itself
It gives everything every time
The right way the way
That says there will be nothing
Left of me tomorrow
Except what appears to be
The beginning of something green
In the otherwise brown fields

Green Peach

Green peach how much rain
Must you bear on this journey
Before sweetness comes

To Draw A Mountain

You need
Only paper
And ink

It may be
One mark
On the otherwise
Blank surface

Pointed upward
Or flat topped

There are no places
Where birds are not welcome

You may place a tree
Here or there
But you do not want
To see a forest

Somewhere we know
Water is moving
Toward us

You may be able
To hear it
Or even smell
Its clean smell
But we cannot
See it falling

Near the bottom
You may put
A person

Or two
Who
Like us are blind
And feeling
Their way home

Singing

"true singing is about nothing" Rilke

Sometimes I sing and singing comes
From my mouth and from my body
I sing like there are strangers at the door
I sing like paint poured out on the floor
I sing like standing in line for tickets
Like a man with three shirts on
Singing like I am seven hours
From Buffalo or some other place
Where deep snow falls
I am singing like a man
Stuck on the back steps
Of a building as the snow falls
In the deep woods of my song
And singing pours out of my body
Out of my hands
Out of my outstretched arms

Wolf

There is a wolf
Outside my door
That consists
Of all the things
I have forgotten

See how it circles
In that familiar pattern

Watch it lay its head
Back and howl
Like a hungry child

And those teeth
Are the many
Small knives
With which I
Have caused pain
To myself and others

A Kind of Defense

It was a kind of move
A kind of defense
Hiding what was worthless
So the thieves could steal
Everything of value
I didn't know any better
I practiced the words
Over and over again
They still refused
To come out in order
They were like
Those two geese we saw
On the ride to Columbus
Not enough to form a letter
And the sound they made
Only went in one direction
I could not call out
To anyone who could hear
My words flew off
Into the darkness
It was winter
They needed to be
Someplace warmer
I was alone
And left silent

Bringing Home Strange Goods

When I look around
At all the things
I have I think
Of Joseph's brothers
Returning home
After selling him
To the caravan
Traveling to Egypt
How their father
Would have been concerned
About where they found
The strange goods
They brought home
Had he not been
Distracted by the grief

Incarceration

Like solving old crimes
With new technology
I found I have had
The wrong criminals
Locked up all these years

Their lives like ours
Spent in the wrong places

And like us
Finally free
From all those
Wrong ideas
They are not bitter
But rejoicing
As they walk
Out into the street

Convention

It was as if I had stumbled
Into a convention of dreamers
I could not tell how long
They had been convened
Nor was it clear from their calendar
Of events how long they would be at it
All the great dreamers were there
Joseph retelling as he had
To his jealous brothers his dream of stars
And that boy from Mrs. Phelps third grade class
Who never returned after thanksgiving break
He was telling how after he found the words
Alone in the moonlight he had never been able
To put them back together again
No word was willing to lead the others
Into a greater meaning
And no matter what order
He placed them in each sentence
Became harder and harder to understand

II

I Believe

I believe in a city that
Talks to itself a city
With three faces like
The dancers that come home at dawn
Three cities and a river and
A false light in the eye of the poor
Where love comes down from
The roof tops at noon
And is greater than the sum
Of its pieces

Walrus

It slips from my heart
Like the walrus slips
From the ice into the sea
Diving deep to dig for oysters
In the mud with its ivory tusks

But it always returns

I feel those wet flippers
And the pain from two huge tusks
Pulling that dark slippery wrinkled form
Back onto my heart
And I am frightened
Until I feel the warmth from its blubber
Which the Eskimos eat
And burn in their lamps
And I want to live and receive light
From it too

I shake again
When the walrus moves
Knowing it is hungry
And must go
I cry wait
As it slides into the water
And I hope for the day
When my arms
Will be strong enough
To wrap around and hold
The broad neck
Of this mustached whale horse
To ride it into the dark
Into the warmer water
To dig in the mud and watch
For polar bears and kayaks

Something You Might Like

Here is something you might like
He said showing her the brochure
A calm sea with whales breaching

Or this one with the white beaches
He thought she wanted to get away
She thought he only thought about getting away

But he left the door open
He would settle for a drive upstate
Where rumors of autumn swirled

He could wait until she was ready
Whatever that meant he had waited before
When she wanted to eat only Indian food

He waited through the heat which he didn't mind
And through the various curries he waited
While she tried several varieties of rice

Before settling on one which took a long time to soften
He was hungry he told her and not always patient
And she wanted to hang photos

Of the foothills of the Himalayas in the living room
Where he wanted the girls in bright dresses
Who were dancing in front of the temple

Love Song

When we come together
I like to think of Einstein
Of energy and mass
And the speed of light squared
And what makes the hair
Go white and wiry

Tonight

What comes
From the darkness tonight
A few wispy clouds
In the waning moonlight
And the river
As it continues
Its long conversation
With the sea
A true journey
It has seen so much
And the sea
Longs to hear
Every detail

At Night

After you put the book down
Turn off the little light
That sits nearest the bed

After the patient part
As the body begins its rest
And is lured to sleep
By the gentle rocking
Of nights waves and you
Push the little boat
Out onto the dark water
Where the other disciples
Have promised to meet

The wind does what it does
On nights like this

And you step out
Walking a little further
Into the trusting arms
Of the water until each night
Is a furthering of your faith
A gathering of what you desire

Remember

"…let her breast satisfy thee at all times…" Proverbs 5:19

Remember your breasts
How they hung there
Staring into the future

Remember how the curtains parted
As the warm wind crawled
Through the open window in august
As you came dripping from the shower
Water wanting everything wet

Remember third grade
How smart they were
Even at that young age

Remember how well behaved
They were that summer
We drove through the Bible belt
The perfect travelers

Remember how you bent at the waist
Naked swaying gently
Left to right to left

Remember how they sat
With you in the garden
Among the carrots and the cucumbers
The summer the pears were so sweet
Those orange socks you wore
The songs we played for them

Remember how they listened
As we took turns reading
Dante's Inferno all summer

They were like two mystics
Praying on the side of a mountain
As the angels rejoiced

Or two reckless teenagers
Learning to drive
Hitting the brakes and swerving
Just in time
Leaving the instructor amazed
Astonished and afraid

Remember how patient they were
Like two fishermen
Waiting for the first fish
Dreaming of dinner
Pan fried over an open flame

Two flames flickering in the darkness

Two goats tethered to the shore
Under the moonlight

Two birds that have flown
From their cages
But who have not forgotten
How to sing

Hummingbird

Have you watched
The hummingbird
In his morning rounds
As he whispers his secret
In the ears of the flowers

We know it is a sweet story
He tells for they have come
All the way from nothing
Wearing their bright dresses
To hear what he has to say
And he who cannot wait to tell
Vows to visit every day

Joy

I let the bee stand for joy
How in its holometabolism
It becomes something
Other than what it was
With its clear insect blood

I let the bee stand for joy
Because solitary or queen of a colony
It is always herbivorous

I let the bee stand for joy
Because led by the desire for sweetness
It is always ready to learn

And I let the bee stand for joy
Because its honey stomach
Is larger than its brain
Or its tube like heart

I let the bee stand for joy
Because it could not exist
Without the flower

Gone

Don't look for me
When you come
To the mountains
I am not there
In spite of what
My letters said
Those are not my things
Laying around the dark pit
And those little songs
Tied to the trees
With golden thread
Are just fruit
For a certain bird
That no longer hunts
It just sits
In that scraggy tree
And sings

Blind

What difference do the stars make to the blind
We who must handle everything we believe in
Who must touch the unseen to have faith
There was a woman separated like us from the others
Yet she knew to touch was to be made whole
She could overcome such great distances
As the stars are from us in an instant
By reaching out in the darkness
By touching the garment of night

Signal

I cannot say for certain
What secret signal they send
But the bee is there
When the flower needs it
Again and again and again

This Day

I dedicate this day to you
For your listening pleasure
Let's have some birds
Whispering to one another
But loud enough for you to overhear
May the bees stimulate your flowers
May many frogs splash into your pond
And if the wind decides to carry
A fragrance past your place
Let it be the summer wind
Let it arrive like a letter
Mailed by a forgotten friend
Who has made a marvelous
Discovery in the mountains
And wants you to be
The first to know

Forgotten

I wanted to take the beer with me
I wanted the whiskey too
I wanted to be alone awhile
I wanted to forget
I did not know why the moon
Kept one side hidden from me
I did not know if it was something I did
Or if it was something I said
Or even less like something I thought
Or less still like something I failed to think
I could not see her sitting in her dark house
I could not touch her there could not
Comfort one who was so far away
She might be forgotten

Faintly

The old man
Had a face
Soft like a dove
He stood
Looking down
At an old photo
Of a building
Which no longer stands
In front of which
Two women were dancing
Who no longer dance
And faintly
As faint as light
From a long dead star
You could hear him cooing

Love Makes No Promise

Love makes no promise to be easy
It promises to tear from your fields
By the roots the weeds
That have been clouding your mind
To move those immovable stones
That cause you to stumble so awkwardly
Promises to reduce you to nothing
So what grows back will be pure
Shining like a field of lilies
That the dew has touched just at sunrise

She Was Never Shy

Sometimes when the wind died down
And the waves were acting less heroic
She would talk about it in a way
You could understand for awhile
It had to do with the two of them
And where they had been on hot nights
And how they had been able to come through
It together in a way that made them less separate
Less willing to accuse less aware of the city
And what went on while they were longing
To be with one another

Something Is Happening

It can compress itself
And fit inside a walnut shell

Or expand into
What is large enough to hold it

The universe itself
Keeps expanding

But I have been thinking lately
About autumn

How the world allows
That one brief moment of passion

How it throws off its red and yellow scarves
Revealing nothing which must be why

The world allows this display
The world which usually demands

A plainness an unwavering choice
Admits for one moment

That the color of these things drifting
Is the way it is suppose to be

I know the angels are hierarchical
With one above the world

And one above each people
And one above each person

And I think in autumn it must be possible
To go straight to the top

With color and abandon
To drift for that one afternoon

On a hillside overlooking the valley
Where everything is occurring

In its mundane way
While out here in the wind

Something remarkable is happening

Blueberry

Have you ever found yourself
In a blueberry patch
Somewhere in a back pasture

Just you alone among the berries

And life itself
Is suddenly sweet
And round and ripe

Still Life With Yellow Apples

Five apples in a green bowl
They illuminate the dark month
They smell like summer

These five are the world
Their black seeds have
Hidden orbits these apples
Are apples they are hung in space
Surrounded by the great green wall
Of the bowl

Like a gathering of old men
Who talk about the sun
They speak softly
About the true center the core

Here
In this bowl
The world begins again
Here in this bowl nothing
Here in this bowl everything remains
The same

Five yellow mountains
With black birds and clouds

Daily Bread

I am not one
For casual conversation
I can't just ask
The baker
If the bread is fresh

I want to know
How many times
He touched it

What he hugged
The flour in

How the wet
And dry ingredients
Reacted when
They realized
They were no longer
Separate but mixed

And if he had
To call the yeast
Like Lazarus
To get it to rise

Or if it rose by itself
And if he can bear
To part with this loaf

When I Called Out To You

When I called out
Underneath the tired
Limbs of the ancient oak

When I called under
The low hanging
Branches of the pine

From a place
That smells of the night
That smells of love
In the night

When love called
Underneath the low
Hanging branches of heaven
It was night

And I
In my loneliness
Answered

Rome

Sitting in the park waiting while two cats,
The cats of Rome, fought over an old cheese sandwich.
Waiting back then when waiting was all I had, when
I thought forgiveness was a well where the poor
Gathered and love was a bath with rose petals and doves.
How confused I was then. Even though I was poor
My poverty was not enough, back then, when I confused
Loss and love, not knowing they always walked together.
I don't recognize my life then in those clothes, when
I thought the body was star shaped not diamond shaped.
I didn't even know how beautiful the body could be.
I didn't know what was harmful and what wasn't.
Or how pain could be physical and not just being
Alone in the darkness. Or how a simple human act
Could turn me around on that lonely path.
How, left on the outskirts of town
Without any maps, I took the only road that mattered.
I know now that it was the way out even though I couldn't
See it then. Even though I couldn't see how things so broken,
Irreparably broken, could be the unexpected turn that made
Everything alright again. That made a world struggling
For breath in the middle of the night able to go on.

Hunted

The inattentive hunter
Does not notice the deer
Slipping quietly
Beneath his tree
As the fisherman
Who ignores the tiny tug
Can lose a catch
So we who fail
To feel a kindness
Swimming through
Are not kind
And the deer
Nibbling out of love
For the fresh green leaves
Can walk out
Of our lives leaving
Only a great longing

The Rain

Remember that summer
We decided to immerse
Ourselves in the music
Of Mozart how I called you
My Amadeus and I was your wolf
Or sometimes your fox
But mostly your prodigy
Remember the taste
Of the watermelon we ate
While listening
To his third symphony
And how majestic
That red juice was
As it ran everywhere
And how I hated
It on my hands
And the rhythmical
Manner you developed
Disposing of the seeds
How even the birds
That summer seemed
To be singing something
You had first heard in him
Even the traffic
Outside Chattanooga
Seemed to be
Envisioned before by him
And how wandering
In an obscure field
You felt we had been
Remembered by him before
We happened to be here
And how we knew then
That those notes

Helped bring us to
This hillside where
Everything we looked out on
Was like music and we realized
Like the rain he had
Enough notes to cover everything

Horizon

The sky has fallen
Into the sea this morning
As if the two old lovers
Had traveled all this way
To tumble together
And now cannot keep
The rain from falling

I Want To Be Your Lover

I want to be your lover

I want to fill in all the holes
To find you complete
Wanting nothing but my love

We will wade into the water together

The circles that wading sends
Will be enough
Will last and last
Like memories people have
Of times when nothing was wrong
When everyone they knew
Was happy for the same reasons
Celebrating together

I want to be your lover
In that seamless way
That water has
Always finding what it wants

I want to be the story you tell
That means different things
To different people

The story of how I am your lover
And there would be no end

I want to love you
Like the big trucks

Love the highway
We would be
In another state by morning

I could say
I love you
But that is not enough

I could say the owl
Loves the night
But you know that
When you hear
It calling your name
All night

Like the owl
My eyes have learned
To see you
In all your darkness

Like the owl
I can hear
The little things stir in the night

The little things you love
Those are the things
I want to bring you
When I slip
Into your tent
At night
Like your lover

ABOUT THE AUTHOR

GERRY GRUBBS

Gerry Grubbs was born, raised and still lives in Cincinnati, Ohio. He has poems appearing in or forthcoming from Poet Lore, Painted Bride Quarterly, and Mudfish, among other magazines. He has been the Poet Laureate of the Olympic Garage since 2005.

BOOKS BY DOS MADRES PRESS

Michael Autrey - From The Genre Of Silence
Paul Bray - Things Past and Things to Come
Paul Bray - Terrible Woods
Jon Curley - New Shadows
Deborah Diemont - The Wanderer
Joseph Donahue - The Copper Scroll
Annie Finch - Home Birth
Norman Finkelstein - An Assembly
Gerry Grubbs - Still Life
Richard Hague - Burst, Poems Quickly
Pauletta Hansel - First Person
Michael Heller - A Look at the Door with the Hinges Off
Michael Heller - Earth and Cave
Michael Henson - The Tao of Longing
Eric Hoffman - Life At Braintree
James Hogan - Rue St. Jaques
Keith Holyoak - My Minotaur
Burt Kimmelman - There Are Words
Richard Luftig - Off The Map
J. Morris - The Musician, Approaching Sleep
Robert Murphy - Not For You Alone
Robert Murphy - Life in the Ordovician
Peter O'Leary - A Mystical Theology of the Limbic Fissure
David A. Petreman - Luz de Vela en Quintero
David A. Petreman - Candlelight in Quintero
David Schloss - Behind the Eyes
William Schickel - What A Woman
Murray Shugars - Songs My Mother Never Taught Me
Nathan Swartzendruber - Opaque Projectionist
Jean Syed - Sonnets
Madeline Tiger - The Atheist's Prayer
Henry Weinfield - The Tears of the Muses
Henry Weinfield - Without Mythologies
Tyrone Williams - Futures, Elections

www.dosmadres.com